WILLIAM M. GAINES'S

POLYUNSATURATED

Albert B. Feldstein, Editor

WARNER BOOKS

A Warner Communications Company

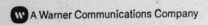

Recently, we asked a group of "Surfing" enthusiasts what makes their sport so great. They looked us over with contempt and answered that we were "too old to dig!" *Too old?* US?! Well, we packed a lunch and headed for the beach. We were determined to find out just what it was that anyone saw in "Surfing". Was it the fresh salt air? Was it the bright warm sun? Was it the soft clean sand and the roaring sea? Was it the hordes of healthy young bronze-skinned beach bunnies in teensy-weensy Bikinis? The answer was obvious: It was the fresh salt air and the bright warm sun and the soft clean sand and the roaring sea! Who *said* we were *too old?* HAH!! So now, we'd like to share what we found out with you in this MAD close-up on . . .

SURF-ING

ARTIST: GEORGE WOODBRIDGE   WRITER: AL JAFFEE

THE STUNNING
PANORAMA OF SURFING

This is the breathtakingly beautiful tableau that greets the on
athletes balance gracefully on their boards, and glide silentl

No ballet scene, that is, except maybe one of those gang-war
seems like every young clod who has ever seen an Annette
thinks he can be a Surfer . . . and this is what "Surfing" is

oker at a Surfing beach, as a line of daring young
on a sparkling wave. No ballet scene can match it!

ance sequences from "West Side Story!" Mainly because it
'unicello "Beach Movie" or heard a "Beach Boys" record
eginning to look like with all those maniacs out there!

AN ILLUSTRATED GLOSSARY OF SURFING TERMS

Before going any further with this article, it will be necessary for the reader to familiarize himself with the Surfer's private language. There is a definite purpose in this language. It was not created for any of the square reasons that many Clubs or Fraternal Organizations have for their mumbo-jumbo. It was not created just to have a silly secret language. The reason for Hip Surfer Talk is more serious and meaningful than that. It's to show off!

"GREMMIE"

A beginning Surfer. Easily recognized because they're the ones who mostly use the idiotic words on this page.

"HO-DAD"

A refugee from the drop-out motorcycle set who takes up Surfing. Easily recognized because they can only dig the pictures on this page.

"DING"

What happens when your surfboard hits something hard.

"BING"

What happens when the something hard your surfboard hits hits you right back.

"ALL-TIME"

A great surf! For example, Hawaii's surf is always all-time! California's surf is often all-time! Arizona's surf is never all-time!

"TAKING GAS"

Losing control and going down — not to be confused with stealing fuel from a parked car to get to beach.

"BULLY"

A big bronze-skinned Surfer who carelessly kicks sand when he walks on the beach.

"SKINNY"

A weak pale-skinned Surfer who usually gets all of the sand kicked by the Bully.

"DOWN"

What happens to a Surfer after "taking gas." He is underwater and is expected to reappear momentarily.

"DROWN"

What happens to a Surfer after "taking gas." He is underwater — not expected to reappear momentarily.

"SAND"

Found in every orifice and pore of a Surfer's body, it makes a gritting sound when he chews or blinks his eyes.

"VAVAVOOM"

A beach bunny who goes off with the Bully, leaving the Skinny—while everyone else wonders what she saw in the Skinny in the first place.

"PUKA"

This is not what a Surfer becomes when the waves go down and up and down and— It's a break in the surface of the board. Not serious.

"COMPOUND FRACTURE"

A break in the body of the Surfer. Also not serious. Unless it's a break in the body of the board. Then it is serious. Only then, it is called a compound puka.

"BIG MAN"

A Surfer who carries his board around during non-surfing weather to give the impression he's hardy.

"WIPE OUT"

To lose a wave. Also what Surfers will probably do to the MAD Magazine offices when they see this article.

MANEUVERS

When the Gremmie arrives at the beach, there are two should study the murderous surf and realize that he could decide that it's not too late to quit, and that after a few yellow-bellied coward!" That's lesson #2. But if he's too learn to Surf. The following simple instructions will help

LAUNCHING THE

Wrong Way

Running into surf like this is dangerous, as board could fly loose and kill somebody. Or what's even worse, the board could get a ding.

Paddling into surf is okay, but not if you start in shallow part of surf. Because when wave recedes, you can look pretty ridiculous.

TO LEARN

important lessons he must learn immediately. First, he
get killed out there. That's lesson #1. Next, he should
years, he will get used to being pointed out as "that rotten
chicken for all that, he might as well get out there and
him survive to a ripe old age. Like maybe 24 . . . or 25.

SURFBOARD

Climbing on surfboard
while ignoring waves
is not very pleasant,
unless you feel having
a body full of broken
bones is very pleasant.

Once up, form is very
important—not because
it's safer or better —
but because beach bun-
nies won't look at you
if you do it like this.

Bad form also leads to
other troubles — like
when you hit shallow
water. Then you find
out why sandpaper is
made with beach sand.

Right Way

An experienced Surfer skillfully hurls his surfboard out into sea.

He then gracefully leaps unerringly out onto his surfboard.

He then apologizes for landing on broad instead of on board.

He waits for wave and confidently rides in, thrilling onlookers.

After ride he quickly leaves water to avoid meeting other Surfers.

FANCY STUFF...HANDY TRICKS AND TURNS

THE SPINNER

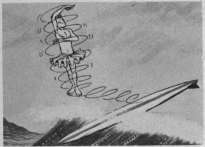

"The Spinner" is a pirouette which is performed while coming in on a wave. It is considered even better, tho, to do it while coming in on a surfboard!

KICKING OUT

"Kicking Out" is moving back on board and losing wave to turn around and go back out again. The move is sometimes used for more than just "showing off"!

WALKING THE NOSE

"Walking The Nose" is strolling over the board while the wave breaks. This Surfer is not walking his nose! He's looking for a contact lens he dropped!

MANEUVERS

HOTDOGGING

A Hotdogger is a character who has no feelings whatso ever for other people at the beach. He weaves in ond out thus causing all kinds of trouble. In the scene above, we see him doing his dirty work. There he is in the lower left dressed in his natty white suit. Next to him is a kid who won't stop screaming until he can get another hot dog. A little further over is a lady who's gagging after biting

OGLING

This maneuver started last year about the same time that the topless bathing suit came out. It is very dangerous for the Surfer who does it, especially if the bunny he's ogling has a big bronze-skinned Bully boyfriend nearby.

TO AVOID

nto her sand-covered hot dog. More to the right are some
rings in the water, marking the spot where a man drowned
after eating four hot dogs and going right in for a swim.
The pimply-faced kid eating his hot dog spends a fortune
on acne medicine, when all the time he's allergic to hot
dogs. Oh, we could go on and on, but we're running out of
space. Besides, we're getting hungry! HEY—Hot Dog Man!!

PILING

This delightful and exciting maneuver was created on the
West Coast for Surfers who are easily bored with ordinary
surfing. After trying it, they are no longer bored. They are
crippled, maimed and disfigured—Yes! But bored—No!

LIGHTNING

This innovation in Surfing was accidentally discovered by a few die-hard Surfers who refused to leave the surf when a thunderstorm came along. Now, when a thunderstorm comes along, there are always a few die-hards who try it.

FREEZING

This maneuver is usually performed well after Summer is over and Winter has set in. It is accomplished by the idiots who refuse to accept the fact that Surfing is over for the season. So they bob around like this till Spring.

Surfing is like drug addiction. A Surfer goes nuts when he cannot surf. But there are many times when he absolutely cannot. The sea may be calm, his board may be broken, or his family may have moved to Kansas City. At these times, a Surfer may start to display severe withdrawal symptoms. His eyes will roll, his stomach will ache and his legs will flap uncontrollably. This has nothing to do with Surfing. He's merely doing some new dance like the Frug. A Surfer who can't Surf simply sits and cries. But now his troubles are over. Inventions are popping up every day to solve his problem. Today, a Surfer can not only get his kicks without a surf, but even without water in some instances.

SURFING WITHOUT A SURF

Boatwake Surfing

A surfer can ride the high fish-tail wake of a powered speedboat all day if he so desires—so long as he does not meet the high fish-tail wake of a powered speedboat coming the other way.

Snow Surfing

This Winter innovation can be just as thrilling as the Summer variety of Surfing. Using a regular surfboard, the Snow Surfer has trees, rocks and annoyed skiers to lend dangerous excitement.

Sand Dune Surfing

Sand Dune Surfing is growing in popularity in arid States. The Surfer rides down dunes until a burning sensation on the soles of his feet tells him that the board has been sanded away.

High Weed Surfing

A Surfer takes his regular Summer beach bunny to find a hill thickly covered with tall weeds. Then, if he is lucky, no idiotic Surfer will disturb him with that stupid High Weed Surfing jazz.

SURFING WITHOUT A SURFBOARD

Body Surfing

This is the same as regular Surfboard Surfing, except that the Surfer's body becomes the board. And repairing the Surfer's body is done the same as with the board, using fiberglass and epoxy.

Skim-Board Surfing

Skim-Board Surfing is performed with a small round disc over the wet flats of a beach. The Surfer jumps onto the Skim-Board—and spins, and skids, and falls on his — well, it takes practice!

Driftwood Surfing

Can be done wherever there's junk on the beach. Just watch the rusty nails, watch the splinters, and mainly watch the beach . . . because driftwood has a tendency to drift out to sea again.

SURFING WITHOUT SURF OR A SURFBOARD

Skateboard Surfing

A Skateboard can be purchased or easily made with a skate stolen from your kid sister. It is ridden almost exactly like a Surfboard: Leaning steers it and nothing stops it. Only when you fall off it, pavement is harder than water.

Teeterboard Surfing

Teeterboard Surfing is very similar to Skateboard Surfing except for one additional thrilling difference: It cannot be done! But that shouldn't really matter to the die-hard desperate Surfing enthusiasts! They all love a challenge!

SURFING'S

SPORTS THAT OVERCAME SERIOUS LIMITATIONS AND HOW THEY DID IT

Fishing

Every lake and stream in the country faced the threat of being fished out until someone came up with the brilliant idea of raising fish artifically and stocking the waters. Now, more money is spent on fishing than any other sport.

SURFING, TOO, CAN GET BIG IF...

ARTIFICIAL SURF-MAKING MACHINES ARE PUT INTO USE ALL OVER!

Then every bay, river, lake, stream, great idea, Surfing lovers, and turn there and surf . . . while we stay skinned beach bunnies. WHO said

LIMITATIONS

The continued growth of Surfing into a big-time sport is seriously hindered by the limited number of good Surfing areas. However, other sports have overcome similar handicaps and gone on to become multi-billion dollar industries.

Skiing

Unpredictable warm spells used to murder this sport and every skiing resort that depended on it. Now, snow can be manufactured artificially and sprayed on slopes, and year-round ski areas are booming from Florida to Calif.

pool and puddle could be used for Surfing. So let's get behind this the whole world into a Surfers' Paradise so you can all get out back on the shore with those beautiful healthy blonde bronze- we're *too old?!*

HOME-SWEET-HO-HUM DEPT.

The "Great American Dream" is to live in peace and harmony with an ideal wife and well-mannered children in an atmosphere that's free from worry and tension. It can't be done, you say? You know of no one who has ever achieved such a euphoric existence? Well, you're wrong! There's a family that lives in bliss week after week! And what's more, it's been doing so for 14 years! We're talking about that happy group of innocents who live completely and hermetically sealed off from reality. We're talking about . . .

THE

ARTIST: MORT DRUCKER

WRITER: STAN HART

Hello, dear. How did things go today?

Terrible. Just **terrible.** First, I pulled the wrong cord on the Venetian blind and the slats went **up** instead of **down.** Then, Art Linkletter's House Party was preempted by a Space Shot. And then, a button worked loose from my cardigan sweater. It's been one thing after another.

NILSON
FAMILY

Harried, why are there **holes** in Oozie's newspaper?

I cut out all the articles that might **disturb** him. If he ever learned about **REAL** problems, he'd **crack up.**

Gee, that's a very good idea.

Not **always.** This year, he's planning a vacation in the **Dominican Republic!**

Hi, Divot. How's the Law Game?

I'm on my way to handle a case right now. Two partners are suing each other and they're waiting for me to do something **idiotic** so they can **forgive** and **forget.** It's nice being a lawyer for nice people. I'm lucky I never handled a case where the people **weren't** nice.

That's right, Divot. Leave the people who **aren't** nice to lawyers like **E. G. Marshall.** And you know how long **he** lasted in television.

Let's look at **home movies,** Dad.

Swell, Rickety. Your wish is my command.

Why do they **ignore me?** Everything around here is **Rickety, Rickety.** Gee, I have no strong opinions, no defined personality, no trace of emotion **either.** I'm everything a Nilson **should be,** yet they turn their **backs** on me. Why? WHY?

BLESS OUR LIVING ROOM

BLESS OUR FOYER

BLESS OUR BLISS

Ever wonder what happens to all the unsold items left on dealers' shelves when the demand for a product fades ... or a craze suddenly dies ... or there was never any demand in the first place? Well, don't look in the garbage dumps for them. Look instead at those little mail order ads in magazines and newspapers—placed by that crafty band of greedy American Businessmen who have discovered

THE WONDERFUL WORLD OF RE-PACKAGING

ARTIST: BOB CLARKE   WRITER: DICK DE BARTOLO

Like f'rinstance, remember the "Hula-Hoop" craze? Suddenly, one day, they zoomed to popularity . . and just as suddenly, one day, nobody wanted to play with hula-hoops anymore. Well, right this minute, manufacturers with millions of hula-hoops in warehouses around the country are thinking of ways to re-package them. So keep your eyes open for these "*new*" products:

WHEN IT COMES TO GAMES, DO YOU ALWAYS LOSE?

IS EVEN PLAYING SOMETHING LIKE TIDDLY WINKS BEYOND YOUR ATHLETIC ABILITY?

THEN THIS NEW GAME IS FOR YOU!

SUPER RING-TOSS

THE GAME YOU SIMPLY CANNOT LOSE!

Features:

TWO HARD-TO-MISS UPRIGHT POLES

SIX EASY-TO-GRASP SUPER RINGS

ONE IMPOSSIBLE-TO-STORE BOX

ONLY **$9.95** PER SET

"SUPER RING-TOSS" REDUCES EYE-FATIGUE — MAKES YOU A WINNER EVERY TIME!   Order yours today from: Circle Industries, Box 80, Round Hill, Virginia

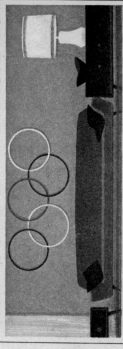

IF YOU THINK THAT'S BAD, HERE ARE SOME MORE PRODUCTS

FROM THE "WORLD OF RE-PACKAGING":

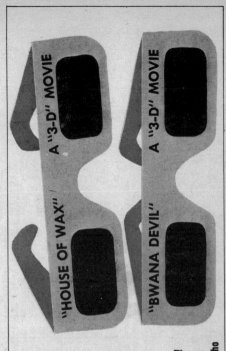

ON THE SUBWAY

In past issues of MAD, you've been exposed to our Academy Awards for home movie buffs, and for parents who drive their kids nuts. But these idiots were strictly amateurs. How about the people who give magnificent acting performances for a living? We don't mean actors who only emote for a couple of hours a day—but the hard-core professionals who perform from 9-to-5 and even longer . . . mainly, The Small Businessman. So just relax, loosen your belts, and watch your pants fall down as we proudly present . . .

THE MAD ACADEMY AWARDS FOR SMALL BUSINESSMEN

ARTIST: JACK RICKARD　　　　**WRITER: STAN HART**

Ladies and Gentlemen . . . welcome to the First Annual MAD Academy Awards for Small Businessmen! Here, in the pot-holed parking lot of the fabulous Swampview Shopping Center overlooking the charming tinder-box homes of the slowly-sinking Jerry-Built Housing Development, we have gathered to honor those people

The first category is in the field of **"CLEANING, PRESSING AND ALTERATIONS."** The nominees are: Dry-Cleaner Abe Prokosh for his marvelous surprise performance in **"Belt? What Belt?!"**—

Mr. Prokosh, I distinctly remember giving you a **belt** with this dress— You must have lost it!

My dear lady—you **wound** me when you accuse me of that! Did I lose the **zipper?** Did I lose the **buttons?** Did I lose the **snaps?** Tell me the truth—did I ever lose anything else?

Well . . . beside the **belt,** you just lost a **customer!**

who owe their success as Small Businessmen to their great acting performances. The winner in each category will receive one of these lovely 14-carat gold-plated statuettes—"The Gimme"!

And now...on with the show!

The second nominee is Tailor Miklos Mulcher for his convincing performance in his famous "Take It From Me, It Fits Like A Glove" routine...

Don't you think you should let it out a little in the front?

But I can't breathe!

Never! Never! If I did that, it would throw a crease across the back!

This is a Saturday Night suit! Do your breathing during the week!

The third nominee is Elmer Budd for his classic **"Look, Lady, I Got My Own Problems"** routine . . .

What do you **mean** my gown won't be ready till Monday!? I need it for **tonight's** Prom!

How should I know that?

But Monday will make **two months** that you've had it—and I paid **extra** for your Special Fast Service!

Two months **IS our** Special Fast Service!

BOSS

RACING FORM

And the winner is Cleaner & Presser Leon Luchow—for his stirring **"I Never Made Any Promises"** routine . . .

I tried, but it's **impossible** to get spots out of silk!

I think it's Orlon!

Orlon! That's the **worst!!**

It might be Rayon!

Rayon! That's even worse!!

Congratulations, Mr. Luchow— and here is your gold "Gimmie"!

Gold!! That's even **worse**!!

The second category is in the field of "SODA FOUNTAINS" —and the nominees are: Oscar Rebus for his "Haven't You Kids Got Anything Better To Do Than Annoy Me" routine . . .

For the millionth time . . . keep your hands off those **magazines**! Who's gonna **buy** them after you mess them up! This ain't the **Public Library**, you know!

We know! The Public Library ain't got magazines with **dirty pictures**!!

The second nominee is Arthur Beemish doing his familiar **"Don't Forget, I'm Watching You"** scene.

You **take** anything without **paying** and I'll call a **cop**! You kids are **all alike** ... juvenile delinquents trying to **rob me blind**! Well, don't try to pull any of that smart-alec stuff around **here** ...

Gee—I just came in to tell you that Mom said you should come home for **dinner**, Pop!

The third nominee is Wolfgang Kuggle for his inspiring performance in **"I Don't Care—That's Not *My* Bottle"** ...

Don't you try and return that deposit bottle **here**! I'm not taking any old bottle you just happen to **dig up**! Besides, I don't **carry** that brand of soda, so don't you try fooling me—

But I'm not **trying** to return it! I'm trying to buy it!

We now come to the **"PHARMACY"** category. The first nominee in this field is Rudolph Phlabb in **"Doctor Knows Best"**...

The second nominee is Alvin Krabb for his brilliant rendition of that old act **"Pharmacy Is A Science"**...

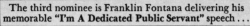

The third nominee is Franklin Fontana delivering his memorable **"I'm A Dedicated Public Servant"** speech . . .

I just moved into the neighborhood and I'm looking for a good drug store!

We are more than a drug store! Consider us your partners in health! We pride ourselves in ethical products and in unwavering service. "Devotion to your needs" is our motto!

Great! When I need medicine, I'll call you!

Fine . . . except after 7 P.M. on weekdays, noon on Saturday, or all day Sunday! We're closed then!!

And the winner of this category is Paul Knitzer for his brilliant performance as **"The Thoughtful One"** . . .

Tut, tut, my dear! Let ol' Doc Knitzer help you **lick** that nasty **complexion** problem! First, my special **skin cream**—only $4.95 a bottle. Next, my special **soap** —only 98¢ a bar. And finally, my special **medicated cosmetic base**—only $3.50 a jar . . .

Thank you so much! I've been so upset!

Well, then—take your mind **off** your problems! How about some **chocolate ice cream**—special today, only $2.50 a gallon?

You were **brilliant**, Mr. Knitzer!

If you give people what they **want**, they'll keep coming back!'

You mean like that **girl**?

As long as she keeps eating that **chocolate ice cream**, she'll keep coming back!

 In the field of **"TV REPAIR,"** the single nominee and winner is Stan Rapier as **"The Very Soul Of Honesty."**

You **thief!** Do you think you can put one **over** on me? I wasn't born **yesterday!**

Control yourself! How can you accuse me of dishonesty? Don't you see my **"TV Repairman's Association Seal"** in the window? Doesn't that motto mean anything? I have a code of ethics to maintain!

But you took out all my **new** tubes and replaced them with **old** ones!

Naturally! Everyone in the business **knows** that they don't make tubes like they used to!

 The next category is **"THE LADIES SHOE SALESMAN."** The single nominee and winner is Barry Frain for his plaintive **"Just A Moment, I'll Be Right With You"**...

Congratulations, Mr. Frain... and here is your gold "Gimmie"...

Oh, dear...everything I've ever won has been in **silver!** Is it possible to have this **dyed to match?**

The next category is **"THE BOWLING ALLEY"** and the single nominee and winner is Stu Grabinsky doing his fabulous **"I Tell You, It's A Perfect Fit"** routine...

Too big? Wouldn't I **know** if those shoes were too big? I've been in this business for 20 years, and this is the first complaint I ever got. If they were any **smaller,** you'd get a **blister!** Ever hear of **Don Carter, the Bowling Champ?** He's about your height and that's the size **he** wears!

Oh, really? In that case...

And he also insists on using a **chipped ball** . . . like **this** one! I'll let you use it, but if Don shows up, you gotta give it back!

VS **SPY**

Not everybody can be a football hero. Not everybody can be a champion golfer or a record-breaking sprinter. Not everybody can be a Mickey Mantle, a Sandy Koufax, or a Pumpsie Green. But just remember: We

FIGHT SONGS for
(Playing the Game

The Sunday Drivers' Cheer
(to the tune of "On Wisconsin")

On you drivers!
  On you drivers!
Inch your way along!
Heading for a Sunday outing—
Fifty million strong (*Stop honking!*)

plain, ordinary, unassuming clods are engaged in the most strenuous, demanding, competitive activity of all —the game of "Everyday Life"! So let's be enthusiastic and strike up the band while we sing these stirring . . .

the COMMON MAN
of "Everyday Life")

See them lined up—
  We will wind up
Home at 10 o'clock!
And to think we only drove
  A-round the block!

ARTIST: GEORGE WOODBRIDGE
WRITER: FRANK JACOBS

The Shoppers' Fight Song

(to the tune of "The Air Force Song")

Off we go
Into the bargain section,
　Running wild
All through the place!
　There's a clerk
Coming in our direction—
　Onward, girls!
Step on his face! (*Clomp-i-ty Clomp!*)
　There's a dress
That we can all fight over—
Grab it, girls! Do not delay!
We'll pull till it's
All torn to bits—
　Rrrrrrrip!
Nothing can stop us shoppers today!

The Taxpayers' Rouser

(to the tune of "*The Song of the Vagabonds*")

On—you big employers,
Clerks, and cooks and lawyers—
Cheat, cheat, cheat
　　Your Uncle Sam!
With expenses padding
And exemptions adding,
Cheat, cheat, cheat
　　Your Uncle Sam!
Don't declare the money that you earn!
Better still—don't file a return!
You'll be saving plenty,
And draw ten to twenty
Years in jail for Uncle Sam!

The Underpaid Employees' March

(to the tune of "Over There")

Get more pay!
  Get more pay!
Make your boss
  Come across!
Get more pay!
For he won't re-fuse you;
He's scared to lose you;
So start de-manding it today!
Don't delay!
  Have your say!
Show your stuff;
  Get real tough;
That's the way!
He's re-fusing!
Your job you're los-ing!
  But you real-ly won;
You got two weeks' sev'rance pay!

The Fat Men's Chorus

(to the tune of *"Stouthearted Men"*)

Give me some men
Who are fat-bellied men
Who will fight for their right to be slim!
Large, hulking slobs
Who will work off their blobs
In a pool, on a track, in a gym—*ugh!*
Grunting and huffing
And wheezing and puffing
They run and they jump and they swim!
When—
They've taken off two pounds
And shout how good they feel,
Then—
Fat-bellied men
Go home and eat a six-course meal!

The Parents' Anthem
(to the tune of "Anchors Aweigh!")

Our kid's away, Thank God!
   Our kid's away!
We've sent him off to camp
At 30 bucks a day-ay-ay-ay—
Though it's a lot to pay
We'll raise no fuss;
If we complain, then they
   Might send him back,
   Might send him back
   To us!

The Song of the Commuters
(to the tune of "When Johnny Comes Marching Home")

We're taking the 5:02 tonight;
   Hoo-rah! Hoo-rah!
We'll work up a hearty appetite;
   Hoo-rah! Hoo-rah!
We're on the train with the special car,
The one that features a stand-up bar;
   And the drinks will pour
   When we take the 5:02!

The Week-End Gardeners' Hymn

(to the tune of *"From The Halls of Montezuma"*)

From the ants in our petunia bed,
　　To the crabgrass on our lawn—
We will fight them off with chem-i-cals,
　　Till the bugs and weeds are gone;
We'll use quarts and quarts of poison spray,
　　And we won't stop till we're through;
All the bugs and weeds are dying now,
　　But the plants and trees are, too!

We're leaving the 5:02 tonight;
　　Hoo-rah! Hoo-rah!
And we're all lit up like a neon light;
　　Hoo-rah! Hoo-rah!
Our wives will meet us and how they'll swear;
They'll call us drunkards, but we won't care,
　　'Cause we feel no pain
　　When we leave the 5:02!

The Consumers' Fight Song

(to the tune of "The Notre Dame Fight Song")

Cheer, cheer for our charge accounts!
    We run up bills in mammoth amounts!
Freezers, sports cars, TV sets—
    Each one is bringing brand-new debts;
What though the bills be great or be small,
    We can't pay one, so why pay at all?
We'll still live in comfort while
    We're heading for bank-rupt-cy!

The Barflies' Hymn

(to the tune of "Over Hill, Over Dale")

Over booze, over beer,
We will argue through the year
As the barflies go yapping along;
Football facts, baseball lore,
We remember every score,
As the barflies go yapping along;
    For it's Hi, Hi, Hee!
When some rummy don't agree—
Shout out your answer loud and strong:
    Sez You!
We will prove our point
While we're busting up the joint
As the barflies go yapping along!

The Tippers' Chant

(to the tune of *"Bless 'Em All"*)

Tip 'em all!
Tip 'em all!
From us they are making a haul!
The cabbie, the waiter,
    the man at the door,
The bellboy, the porter,
    the maid on your floor;
We can't win; so give in; tip 'em all!
They will curse if the sum is too small;
It should be unlawful;
The service is awful;
But we won't look cheap—
Tip 'em all!

THE LIGHTER SIDE OF

SLEEP

ARTIST & WRITER: DAVE BERG

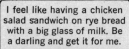

Do you know that **some** people dream in **black and white**, and **other** people dream in **color**?

I dream in **black and white**!

Man, when **I dream**, I dream in **glorious technicolor** on a **wide screen** with **stereophonic sound**. And sometimes, I even have an **intermission** in the middle.

It sounds like you're describing one of those big long spectacular Hollywood movies!

Yep! **That's** where I do my **best sleeping!**

RKO

MOVIES ARE LONGER THAN EVER

Thank you, Arnold. You're such a tiger.

Get lost, Arnold. You're such a pest!

Today, when my Boss told me to straighten up and fly right, I **should** have said . . .

There you **go** again. Every night, before bed, you go through the "**I-should-have-said—**" routine. Do you realize you've got "**20-20 Hindsight**".

I do not!

Ahh, shut up and let me go to sleep.

When she said I've got "20-20 Hindsight", I **should** have said . . .

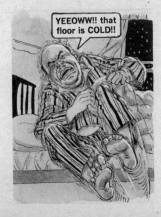

TUNE UP THE VOLUME DEPT.

Nowadays, the Producers of Broadway Musicals are chicken! They're scared stiff of taking chances on new and original stories. Instead, they prefer to play it safe—relying on material that's been tried and proven—like adapting successful stories, novels and plays by world-famous authors. Witness such recent Musicals as "Oliver!" (Oliver Twist by Charles Dickens), "Baker Street" (Sherlock Holmes

by Sir Arthur Conan Doyle), "West Side Story" (Romeo and Juliet by William Shakespeare), "My Fair Lady" (Pygmalion by George Bernard Shaw), Hello, Dolly! (The Matchmaker by Thornton Wilder), and so on and on. Obviously, if this sickening trend continues, we'll be seeing Musicals based on even more unlikely classics. To illustrate, let's follow the bouncing ball as MAD presents four examples of

FUTURE BROADWAY MUSICALS

BASED ON FAMOUS LITERARY CLASSICS

ARTIST : JACK RICKARD   WRITER: FRANK JACOBS

"WHERE'S MOBY?"

Based on "Moby Dick" by Herman Melville

There's Captain Ahab! He's the best Captain on the Seven Seas ... except for one thing—

What's that?

He's insane!

I HEARD THAT! And it's TRUE! I am insane! But I know you'll understand when I tell you why! It's this compulsion I have to find the Great White Whale—Moby Dick!

* I'm as nutty as yesterday's fruitcake!
I'm as jumpy as a fish in a pail!
If you're amazed
That my eyes are both glazed—
It's because of that giant White Whale!

I am balmy, with bats in my belfry!
Lost as a ship that is tossed in a gale!
And if I speak
In a sort of a shriek—
It's because of that giant White Whale!

* Sung to the tune of "'I'm In Love With A Wonderful Guy'"

See him swim my way!
No land-lubber he!
More than seven-hundred-thousand pounds
of blubber he!
I knew all along
That he'd like this song
That I sing to the whale that I love!

And, oh—that glorious thrashing—
As across the ocean he tears!
Although, my boat he is smashing—
I know it's just his way of showing that he cares!

Now I've settled down!
I feel cheerier!
I'll be living out my life
in his interior!
We will sail the brine
Till the time that I'm
Just absorbed by this whale that I love!

"CALL ME JULIUS" Based on "Julius Caesar" by William Shakespeare

Oh, Julius! You've returned from Gaul where you killed 85,000 people and burned their cities! Just listen to the people cheer you for your goodness, justice and love of humanity...

Quiet, my dear! The people are singing the National Anthem!

* Oh, Rome is our dream—
With its wild Colosseum,
And its traffic-jammed Appian Way!
Where the pizza is best—
'Tho it's hard to digest—
And Caesar's king we obey!

Rome! Rome, you're just fine!
With that crazy "S-P-Q-R" sign!
Where the orgies go on
From the evening till dawn,
And each Christian is fed to a lion!

* Sung to the tune of "Home On The Range"

Beware the "Ides of March", Caesar! Brutus and his gang are going to kill you in the Forum!

But Brutus is my second in command! Why should he want to kill me?

Because he's No. 2! He tries harder!

"LOSE YOUR HEAD" Based on "A Tale of Two Cities" by Charles Dickens

* Come on out to the court-yard!
Come on out with the crowd!
We'll have the best rev-o-lution yet!
We'll kill the King and Marie Antoinette!

So let's root, root, root for the Headsman!
He's got a job that is hard!
Yes, it's off—off—off with their heads
At the old court-yard!

Excuse me! I'm Sydney Carton, and this is Lucie Manette! We're just over from London! Could you recommend a good restaurant?

Are you nuts? We're having a revolution! We're killing people by the thousands!

A revolution did you say? Well! My travel agent will surely hear of this!

Do you know where we can find my sweetheart, Charles Darnay?

Darnay? Why we picked him up yesterday! He's in the Bastille . . . . waiting to be guillotined!

* Sung to the tune of "Take Me Out To The Ball Game"

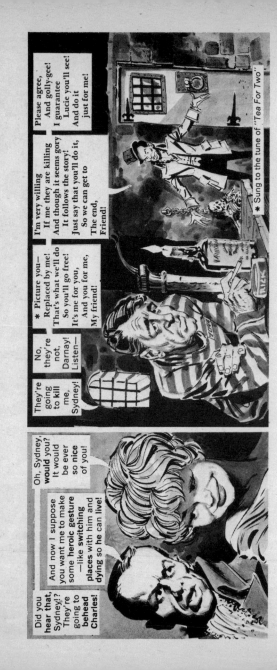

"APE OVER YOU"

Apes! Everywhere I turn—apes! Why can't I lead a normal life like any other sub-human illiterate tree-dweller? Why can't I find a girl who's intelligent and **pretty** for my mate?

Not you, Cheetah! It's true that you're intelligent and pretty —but it wouldn't work! We come from different religious backgrounds!

Ook!
Ook!
Ook!

Based on "Tarzan and the Apes" by Edgar Rice Burroughs

When I feel this way, there's only one thing I can do . . .

* Whenever I get depressed, And start to moon and fret, I let out a jungle scream— Which helps me to forget I've no mate!

While leaping from limb to limb And swinging through the air, I let out a jungle scream— To show that I don't care I've no mate!

I have got a 5-room tree house High above a running brook! It's quite a joint But what's the point When apes can't sew or cook?

If ever I meet a girl, I'll jump and grab her fast! She'll let out a jungle scream— And I will know at last I've a mate!

* Sung to the tune of "I Whistle A Happy Tune"

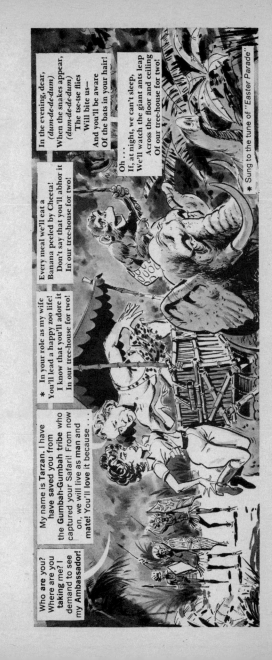

THE PLAY BY-PLAY'S THE THING DEPT.

The latest trend in TV coverage is known as "In Depth" reporting. Those who followed the 1964 Political Conventions know what that means . . . armies of "Anchor Men", "Floor Men", "Local Color Men", and "That's-The-Story-As-It-Looks-From-Here Men" interviewing everyone in sight to get the "Full Story". Because this type of coverage proved successful, it won't be long before unimaginative network big-wigs decide to turn these squads of reporters loose in other areas of television. F'rinstance, MAD now presents a preview of what to expect in one of the many areas that *does not need* this type of coverage, and so *will probably get it!* Mainly, here is . . .

FOOTBALL "IN DEPTH"

ARTIST: GEORGE WOODBRIDGE

WRITERS: RONALD AXE & SOL WEINSTEIN

Mel, I couldn't have said it better myself! It certainly **is** a beautiful, crisp, cool day here at Rocket Stadium ... really great football weather! But let's see what it looks like to **John Hunt** down on the playing field ...

GWOODBRIDGE

This is John Hunt, your **10-to-20 Yardline Reporter!** Just seconds ago, I asked coach **Albie Vermin** what kind of a football day it looked like to **him!** And here's his answer ... recorded just moments ago—thanks to the miracle of video tape ...

It seems we're having a little **technical difficulty** down there, but we'll bring you that tape as soon as our engineers have it cleared up. **Charlie?**

Well, Mel, it looks to me as though we've had a little **technical difficulty!** Interestingly enough, while we were trying to **show** you that tape, the Hawks kicked off to the Rockets! But for **that** story let's switch to **Ward Ellis** down on the playing field . . .

Fans, as Charlie Dittoe just reported, and I can confirm it from here, the Hawks **have** kicked off! The ball was taken at the Rocket five yard line! But the **unusual** thing was the **height** of that kick! I don't believe I've **seen** a football go so high in my fifteen years of announcing this great game of pro football! Anyhow, that's the way the kickoff looked from here! Now, back to the booth . . .

Thanks for that penetrating analysis of **Groza Spinoza's kick**, Ward!

That sure was a **high kick** by Number 88, Groza Spinoza. Incidentally, while Ward was **bringing** that report to us, Rocket halfback Max Shnell ran the kickoff back for a **touchdown**! Joe "the Toe" Williams then **failed to kick the extra point**—the **first time** that's happened in his career!

And **what** a career it's been for Joe! All-State at Ridley High, 3 years All-American at I.C.U. and 7 years a great star for the Rockets . .

Mel, pardon me for **interrupting** this interesting sidelight on Joe "the Toe", but there seems to be some **excitement** down on the field! To sum it up, Jim Ozi threw a 90 yard pass to Frank Guffaw who made a sensational catch to **tie up the game**! Then, Paul Hornmeister's **conversion kick** gave the Hawks **the lead** . . . sorry to cut in, Mel!

That's okay, Charlie! I see that the Rockets are now in their huddle with fourth down and 3 yards to go for a score! So let's go to our **Huddle Man, Jim Sony,** for that story . . .

I'm down here in the Rocket huddle where they've just called a "Quarterback Sneak"! This could really catch the Hawks off guard . . .

". . . could really catch the Hawks off guard . . .

You heard it, guys— **QUARTERBACK SNEAK!!** Let's **KILL 'EM!!**

Well, Finn Starr has just worked his way into the **record books!** This is only the **third** time in a Hawk-Rocket game that a quarterback has broken both legs on a 4th down, 3 yards-to-go situation! If Finn were **conscious** now, he'd be a very **proud young man!**

Hate to change the subject, Mel, but during the past few minutes there's been a lot of **scoring** down there by both sides! And if I'm not mistaken, this is the **kind** of thing that may well decide the **outcome** of this game—not to mention the **championship!** With just seconds left to play, let's go down to **Hank Wilson** . . .

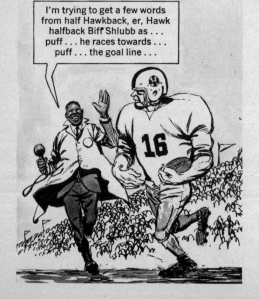

BZZZZZT

John, in answer to that question, I just want to say that, in my personal opinion, it looks like a beautiful crisp, cool, great day for a football game . . .

M**NITOR 3**

Well, that was the interview we tried to bring you earlier when we developed technical difficulties! But now, thanks to the miracle of video tape, you finally saw it!

That's right, Mel! And incidentally, while you were watching it, the last play of this crucial Championship game was concluded! Biff Shlubb, charging toward the goal line . . .

And, I should add right now, Charlie, that this was only the fourth time in the history of this league that a 175-pound halfback of Polish extraction . . .

Gee, Mel, I hate to interrupt, but do we have time for the final score?

I'm **afraid not**, Charlie! There's just enough time to tell our listeners that this **"Football In Depth" Presentation** featured Anchor Men Charlie Dittoe and yours-truly Mel Hyndsite—Produced by Howard Cunningham—Directed by Nigel Evans—Statistical Research by Jethro Abney—our Men-On-The-Field were John Hunt at the 10 yard line, Ward Ellis at the 20, Arnold Stone at the 30, Kenny Levitz at the . . .

Here we go again with the game in which we take ordinary Dictionary words, and dream up some kookie animals that these words suggest. Mainly, here we go with

THE RETURN OF THE

MAD

superficial

romantic

BEASTLIES

ARTIST: PAUL COKER JR.　　　**WRITER: PHIL HAHN**

billy club

Araby

threadbare

sourdough

humdinger

ordain

first aid kit

Good Housekeeping Seal

Balboa

Bangkok

bum steer

crochet

HEY, KIDS! EVERY YEAR, ALONG ABOUT

. . . start getting on your nerves?

. . . and act bored?

SPRINGTIME, DO YOUR PARENTS . . .

. . . make impossible demands?

"CAMP

MAD'S
Summer
For

ARTIST: PAUL COKER JR.

HERE ARE SOME OF THE
MAD'S SUMMER CAMP

Transportation To and From The Camp

Let's go, Senior Adults! Line up here in size place!

Hey, I should be in **front** of him!

No—with adults, it's size place according to **stomach** sizes!

Take care of yourself, Dad, Don't forget to write! Dress warm! And drink your Metrecal!

SUMMER? PACK THEM OFF TO ...

"ALFEENEUMAHAHA"

Camp Adults

WRITER: LARRY SIEGEL

WONDERFUL THINGS THAT FOR ADULTS HAS TO OFFER:

See what you did, Mother! You **rushed** me so much today, I forgot to sew a **name tag** on your girdle!

Stop crying! Before you know it, Summer will be **over**, and Dad will be **home!**

I can't **help** it! He's only 37 . . . and he's never been away from home before!

All Kinds Of Competitive Sports

A Well-Equipped Infirmary

A Magnificent Lake

Arts and Crafts

A Camp-Reunion at a
Mid-Town Hotel Next Winter

There is a new retail shop that is beginning to blight our landscape—the Greeting Card Store. Inside, you can pick out all sorts of messages to send. However, you'll have to search long and hard to find the corny, sentimental cards of yesteryear. Today, the Greeting Card Industry has gone "clever". Who is the diabolical genius behind this movement? Well, let's drop in on the biggest "Card Shark" of 'em all as

MAD INTERVIEWS THE GReeTING CaRD MANUFaCTUReR OF THE YEAR

ARTIST: JOE ORLANDO   **WRITER: STAN HART**

Hi, MAD fans. I'm **Frank Giffurd**, talking with **Mr. Konrad Kupid**—President of the "Klever Kard Kompany"! Tell me, Mr. Kupid, what are the distinguishing features of the modern greeting card?

Lousy art, infantile hand-lettering, and ridiculously high prices!

And this makes you angry?

No—this makes me **rich**! That's the kind I put out!

I don't understand! Don't people send cards to express **affection**?

Silly boy! People send cards because they're **coerced** into it! Therefore, they begin to **dislike** the people they **HAVE** to send cards to! Klever Kards kill two birds with one stone! They discharge **obligations** and **hostilities** at the same time!

In here, we have my writers! I see we're in luck! They're just about to test a new card idea on our One-Woman Panel of Experts!

WRITERS PRIVATE

POW!

Ah—a "Mother's Day Card"! How do you like it?

YOU'RE NOT LIKE OTHER MOTHERS

YOU HAVE ABSOLUTELY **NO** MaTeRNaL iNSTiNCT!

I guess mothers today don't expect something warm and loving!

Mothers today don't even **deserve** something warm and loving!

What **other** cards do you make?

Well, we've just finished printing our "Thank You" Cards—and now we're starting our "You're Welcome" Cards!

And after that?

We'll do our "Thank You For Your 'You're Welcome'" Cards! We cover all bases!

That's amazing!

Today, people have become so **compulsive** about sending cards that they can't even **wait** for a special occasion. In fact, it's kind of an **"In"** thing to find a **new clever card** to send! So we have to keep coming up with them—like **this** one!

i HAD A SPaRE MiNUTe
...SO i THOUGHT ABOUT ALL YOUR GOOD QUALITIES!

So for a **quarter**, a person can feel **clever**! Of course, if he were **really** clever, he wouldn't **have** to spend a quarter on a card to come up with something smart!

"Graduation Cards", eh? I guess these are seasonal—only sold at **Graduation** time in June!

Nonsense! There are Graduation Days every day of the year—like these . . .

Congratulations On Graduation From Your **CHA-CHA LESSONS!**

Now ... Watch Your Step!

Congratulations On Your Graduation

From ... A Chevvy to A Buick!

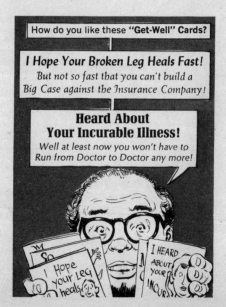

A DREADFUL DAY

THE LIGHTER SIDE OF... SUMMER EVENINGS

WRITER & ARTIST: DAVID BERG

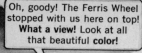

Oh, goody! The Ferris Wheel stopped with us here on top! **What a view!** Look at all that beautiful **color!**

The midway is bathed in a rainbow of red and yellow lights! The people look like Ken and Barbie dolls dressed in blue and gold doll clothes!

From here, the landscape looks like it's been painted by brushes dipped in various shades of purple! The cars look like tiny black toys moving across grey cardboard roads, feeling their way with white fingers from pencil-flashlight headlights!

And even **you** . . . Lenny . . .

YOU'RE SUCH A LOVELY SHADE OF **GREEN!!**

Look at that! She **beat** me by **six strokes!** Boy, if this isn't a classic example of a dumb broad making her date feel like an **idiot** and never getting dated by him **again!**

Oh, Steve, darling! I think it was so **sweet** of you to **deliberately let me win!**

Hmmmmm! I wonder what she's doing **next** Saturday night??

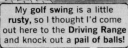

My golf **swing** is a little **rusty**, so I thought I'd come out here to the **Driving Range** and knock out a **pail of balls**!

PAIL OF
BALLS
50¢

POT

Boy! Invite a bunch of teenage boys to a backyard barbecue and under cover of darkness, they turn out to be nothing but **animals**!

Men are **all alike**! All they want to do is satisfy their **primitive urge**!

You'd think girls were made for nothing else but **that**!

They're **all hands and mouth**!

It's **disgusting**! They're interested in **one** thing, and one thing **only**!

FOOD!

Wow! When you come out, it hits you like a **blast furnace!**

I'll say! I forgot how **hot** it was outside!

Hey, I see you two are just coming out of the movies! How **was** it?

GREAT! On my recommendation, I suggest you **drop** whatever you're doing and **rush** in!

But the critics **panned** it! They said it was **badly written, terribly directed,** and **horribly acted!**

All true . . .

. . . but the performance of the **Air-Conditioning Unit** is worth the price of **admission!**

The **kids** are away at camp, **and** my **wife** is at a **resort hotel** for the Summer—which means my **little one** isn't around to tell me I'm a **failure** because I'm a **Certified Public Accountant** instead of a **Cop!**

My big **daughter** isn't around to blame me because I can't afford to send her to a **fancy status college** like Vassar!

And my wife isn't around to tell me I'm getting **bald** and **pot-bellied!**

So what are you **complaining** about? You should be **happy!** Nobody's around to **insult** and **abuse** you!

That's just the **trouble! I MISS IT!**

MAD'S

PUZZLE

PUZZLES @ RIDDLES :
* BRAIN-TWISTERS :*
REBUSES @ POSERS
@ CROSSWORDS @
INANITIES ☆ AND
OTHER TIMEWASTERS

ARTIST & WRITER: AL JAFFEE

ONE REASON THIS NEW FEATURE WAS CREATED IS BECAUSE *MAD* READERS ARE BRILLIANT, INTELLIGENT YOUNG PEOPLE WHO MIGHT ENJOY SOMETHING CHALLENGING LIKE THIS. ANOTHER REASON IS THAT THEY ARE ALSO LAZY SLOBS, AND DOING THESE PUZZLES IS ABOUT AS EASY AS LOUNGING AROUND WATCHING *TV* ALL DAY.

COLORING
CORNER

THIS IS THE BEAUTIFUL AND COLORFUL *BOUGAINVILLEA PLANT.* CAN YOU GUESS HOW TO COLOR IT? *(SEE ANSWER BELOW)*

ANSWER

COLOR IT *DEAD!* ANY IDIOT KNOWS THAT THE *BOUGAINVILLEA* IS A TROPICAL PLANT AND COULDN'T POSSIBLY *SURVIVE* THE HIDEOUS CLIMATE PICTURED HERE !

CONNECT THE DOTS
AND GET A BIG SURPRISE!

IF YOU FOLLOW THE NUMBERS AND CONNECT EACH DOT, A SURPRISE PICTURE WILL APPEAR. YOU'LL NEVER GUESS WHAT IT IS, SO GET RIGHT TO WORK AND SATISFY YOUR CURIOSITY. ALL WE CAN SAY IS THAT WHEN YOU ARE DONE, YOU WILL GET A BIG *BANG* OUT OF IT! IN FACT, IT'S A REAL *KILLER-DILLER!* THE WHOLE IDEA IS HOT AS A *PISTOL!* SO *SHOOT* THE WORKS ON THIS ONE, GANG!

A TRIP TO BRAZIL

CHARLIE FINSTERNICK HAS JUST EMBEZZLED $3,000,000 FROM HIS BANK. SEE IF YOU CAN GET HIM SAFELY TO BRAZIL BEFORE IT ESTABLISHES AN EXTRADITION TREATY WITH THE UNITED STATES, AND WITHOUT RUNNING INTO THESE FIVE TRAPS ALONG THE WAY:

1. WIFE AND SCREAMING KIDS
2. BANK EXAMINER
3. POLICE
4. F.B.I.
5. TEENAGE HOODS HANGING AROUND AIRPORT.

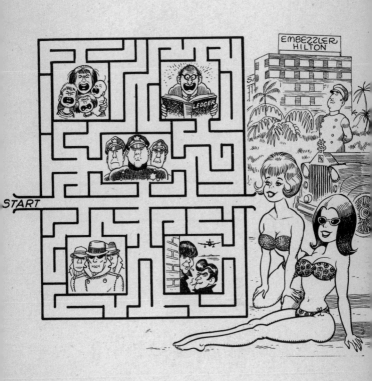

FIND THE NEEDLE

WE'VE HIDDEN A *NEEDLE* SOMEWHERE IN THIS **STACK**! CAN YOU FIND IT? LET'S SEE HOW **SHARP** YOU ARE!

ANSWER : ¡ LOIDI DIAUTS BMUD A 3KIL
LIKE A DUMB STUPID IDIOT!
PILE OF **NEEDLES**! NOW DON'T YOU FEEL
THIS IS NOT A **HAYSTACK**! IT'S A BIG
COULDN'T FIND IT? BOY, ARE YOU BLIND!

OPTICAL ILLUSION

STARE AT THIS BLACK SPOT FOR SIX HOURS WITHOUT BLINKING. THEN TRY TO LOOK UP THE NAME AND THE NUMBER OF A GOOD EYE DOCTOR IN THE PHONE BOOK. YOU WON'T BE ABLE TO DO IT, BECAUSE EVERYWHERE YOU LOOK YOU'LL SEE BLACK SPOTS. YOU MAY ALSO SEE DOUBLE. THIS IS CALLED AN "OPTICAL ILLUSION". AFTER YOU HAVE HAD ENOUGH OF THIS FUN, GET SOME FRIEND TO CALL AN EYE DOCTOR FOR YOU. OTHERWISE, YOU MAY WIND UP WITH THIS EYE TRICK PERMANENTLY!

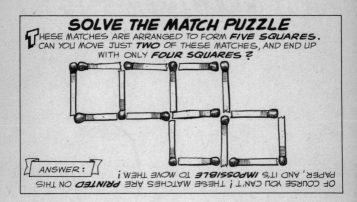

SOLVE THE MATCH PUZZLE

THESE MATCHES ARE ARRANGED TO FORM **FIVE SQUARES**. CAN YOU MOVE JUST **TWO** OF THESE MATCHES, AND END UP WITH ONLY **FOUR SQUARES**?

ANSWER:

OF COURSE YOU CAN'T! THESE MATCHES ARE **PRINTED** ON THIS PAPER, AND IT'S **IMPOSSIBLE** TO MOVE THEM!

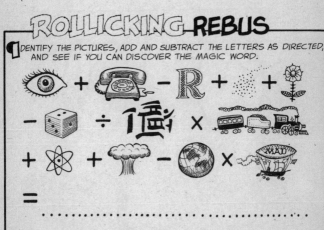

ROLLICKING REBUS

IDENTIFY THE PICTURES, ADD AND SUBTRACT THE LETTERS AS DIRECTED, AND SEE IF YOU CAN DISCOVER THE MAGIC WORD.

IF YOUR ANSWER IS "ANTIDISESTABLISHMENTARIANISM", BETTER CHECK YOUR ARITHMETIC. IF YOUR ANSWER IS "BRTXNTLBE", YOU MADE THE STUPID MISTAKE OF IDENTIFYING THE LITTLE DOTS IN PICTURE FOUR AS "ANTS", WHICH THEY ARE NOT. ACTUALLY, THEY'RE JUST LITTLE DOTS. AND IF YOU SKIPPED DOING THIS PUZZLE ENTIRELY, YOU SHOWED RARE INTELLIGENCE.

HOW TO DRAW GREAT CARTOON LIKENESSES

THIS MONTH'S GUEST ART TEACHER IS THE RENOWNED CARICATURIST, IRVING DRUCKER. SOME OF YOU MAY THINK THAT IRVING'S STYLE IS COPIED FROM ANOTHER "DRUCKER" WHO APPEARS ELSEWHERE IN THIS MAGAZINE. ACTUALLY, IT'S THE OTHER WAY AROUND.

Remember how in the good old days, as soon as an actress reached fifty, she stopped playing glamorous roles and either took nice mature mother parts or she retired? Well, things being what they are today, what with the cost of living and taxes, these old gals can't afford to retire. And there are no nice mature mother parts in movies any more because there's something too disgustingly healthy about nice mothers. So what are "Has-Been Glamour Gals" doing these days? You guessed it! They're making Horror movies! They're discarding their make-up and they're playing maniacs and murderesses. Yes, nowadays "Old Actresses Never Die They Just Hack Away" . . . at each other . . . in movies like this here MAD version, entitled

"HACK, HACK, SWEET HAS-BEEN"

or

"What Ever Happened To Good Taste?"

ARTIST: MORT DRUCKER   WRITER: LARRY SIEGEL

Hello! I'm Cousin Phoebe! Did you get my telegram?

Hi! Ah'm Bubby Jean! Lawsy, Cousin Phoebe, we were so **excited** when you wired you were comin' to visit us kinfolk of yours! Jus' think, the **one relative** that you like **best** inherits **eight million dollars** in your **Will**! Of course, if you cain't make up your li'l ol' **mind**, the **last surviving relative** gets the money, right?

Well, Ah guess **that** should start this li'l ol' sinister plot rollin'!

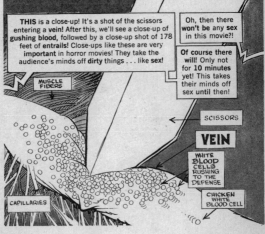

I don't know—as I sit here at the dinner table, I have the sneaking suspicion that the family is trying to butter me up for my money. But then again, I'd hate to be **unfair** to them! Perhaps they eat **all** their meals this way!

Bubby Jean! I just can't take all this horror and death any longer! Look at Selig! He's just **squashed a man, flattened him out**, and now he's **walking all over him!** How ghastly!

You've got it all **wrong!** Selig is just doing another of his **Bofferin TV Commercials!** How do you think we pay the **bills** around here?

YAAAAAHH! Look! It's **Honeybunch!** She's **dead**, and there isn't a **mark** on her! How was she murdered?

See those **empties** all around? It's obvious—somebody fed her 40 bottles of **Pepsi-Cola** . . . and she **burped to death!**

MONTAGE BY SLAVKO VORKAPICH

That's **right**, Bette! You fell for our **trap**! We've **tricked** all you old battle-axes into killing each other off!

But that wasn't **real** killing! That was **trick photography**! Weren't those rubber scissors and **plastic** axes and **wooden** heads and paper maché hands and **ketchup** for blood and . . . ?

No!! Because this morning, **27 of my fellow teenage movie stars** staged a coup d'état at the **Studio Prop Department!** Those were **real** scissors and **real** axes and **real** heads and hands and blood!

Well, it's not fair! All that we of the younger generation want is **what's coming to us!** Mainly —**EVERYTHING!!** Is that asking too much? Well, now we've got it! NOW—WE'VE GOT . . . ugh . . . IT!

Okay! **OKAY!** Quiet on the set of "**DROWN, DROWN, SWEET SURFERS**"! We're going to do the big "**Mass Murder Scene**" now! Places, please, Annette Funnyjello, Pamela Taffy, Bubbi Shaw, Shelley Farblungit and the rest of you! **READY . . . LIGHTS! CAMERAS! MUSIC! DANCING!**

But why kill us old stars off?

Why? I'll **tell** you why! Because we young swingers were monopolizing the industry with **our** movies until you **old broads** came along with **yours!** Everyone **knows** that your **Horror** movies are **just as terrible** as our **Surfing** movies! Still, they call yours **"A" Pictures,** while ours are called **"B" Pictures.** Your movies even get **Academy Award nominations,** while our movies are **ignored** by anyone over sixteen . . .!

It's good to see all those ugly old broads gone now!

The movie industry is no longer dominated by tired, overexposed old bags!

Right! Now it's dominated by us tired, overexposed young bags!

Drown, drown, sweet Surfer;
Surfing now has died!
Get with it, Surfer,
And ride the Horror tide!